STEWART CONN

Ghosts at Cockcrow

BLOODAXE BOOKS

ISBN: 1 85224 686 3

First published 2005 by
Bloodaxe Books Ltd,
Highgreen,
Tarset,
Northumberland NE48 1RP.

www.bloodaxebooks.com
For further information about Bloodaxe titles
please visit our website or write to
the above address for a catalogue.

Bloodaxe Books Ltd acknowledges
the financial assistance of
Arts Council England, North East.

Cover printing by J. Thomson Colour Printers Ltd, Glasgow.

Printed in Great Britain by
Bell & Bain Limited, Glasgow, Scotland.

For Judy,
with love

ACKNOWLEDGEMENTS

Acknowledgements are due to the editors of the following publications where some of these poems first appeared: *Bringing Back Some Brightness: 20 Years of New Writing Scotland* (ASLS, 2005), *Carapace, The Dark Horse, De tots els vents: selected translations of Miquel Desclot* (Angle Editorial, Barcelona, 2004), *Dos Poetes Escocesos a la Mola* (Castellar del Valles, 2002), *Edinburgh Review, Edinburgh Evening News, Envoi, Green Shoots, The Herald, The Interpreter's House, Island, Love for Love* (Pocketbooks, 2000), *Northwords, Orbis, Poetry Cornwall, Poetry Review, Poetry Scotland, Poezija* (Croatian PEN/Croatian Writers Society, Zagreb, 2004), *The Red Wheelbarrow, Scotlands: Poets and the Nation* (Carcanet/ SPL 2004), *The Scots Magazine, Scottish Review of Books* and *Such Strange Joy* (Shore Poets/iynx 2001);

Poems were also broadcast on BBC Radio Scotland and chosen as SAC Poem of the Month (www.scottisharts.org.uk).

Of those who helped directly towards the realisation of this collection I specially thank Serge Baudot, Gerry Cambridge, Anna Crowe and John Purser.

CONTENTS

I

Realm of Possibility

For the plasterers' visit
my study is under dust-sheets;
bookshelves and filing cabinets,

PC and printer, even the special
Robert Burns tankard sent to a jumble sale
which my son winkled

out and brought back saying 'Look
what I've found for you, dad.' Tape deck
and speaker-units, twin snowy peaks,

evoke speeding troikas
abandoning boarded-up dachas
as winter's grip approaches.

Under the billowing drift
stacked poem drafts
wait to be sifted.

In due course I'll note any emergence
from this unseasonal whiteness,
crocus shoots, birds' claw-prints.

Or who knows, discover the spoor
of some elusive creature
and track it to its lair.

In the Garden

What is it about that bush, a *golden choisya*
my wife tells me, which catches the eye –

the abundance of leaves on display
in the sunrise, or the way

these range from lime green
to a lemon glow? This impression

of a nimbus induces some memory
I can't place. Then it hits me:

the Church hymnal
in the manse pew when I was small

bore the imprint of a burning bush, over
the inscription *nec tamen consumebatur.*

This version comes untrammelled
by such baggage. A thrush with speckled

breast struts unecclesiastically
beside it. And that butterfly

I see as more likely to be Li Po
dreaming, than the alter ego

of a Presbyterian divine
sermonising on sin.

Visitation

In pride of place on my work-surface
are an inkwell of weighted glass

and a black quill-pen, presented to me
when I left long-term employ;

a discarded life I heed less
and less, as the years pass.

But every so often with a hoarse *kraaa*
there squats on the sill a hoodie crow,

a gap in one wing where a primary
feather is missing. Teetering raggedly

it fixes me with a bloodshot eye
then flops, disgruntled, away.

Whether intent on repossessing
what belongs to it, or chastising

me for treating its lost quill
simply as a glossy symbol,

I recognise in it the beast
of conscience come home to roost.

The cat meantime sits by the fireplace,
content that nothing is amiss.

American Girl

Having hung for years on my wall
this print, each time I look at it, seems subtly
to have changed: not leaves falling, or the far hill

steepening, no unseasonal powdering of snow
but something scarcely perceptible,
whether an intensifying of the heat-glow

round the racing horse's head, or a brightness
enveloping the straight-backed figure
grasping the reins, whip poised at thirty degrees.

'He is M. Roden,' a slip on the reverse will tell
you, 'driving *American Girl* at Narragansall
Park, Providence, 26th June 1869, a winner all

the way: bought framed, at a mansion house
sale.' Those whirring spokes, slender wheels
puffing up dust-scuts, the whites of the horse's

eyes bursting from their sockets, remain
constants among the trappings of movement.
Yet some element I can't put my finger on

transforms the driver, frozen in his seat,
the glistening filly straining at the bit, hooves
splayed in mid-air. No matter where I sit

or my point of perspective on the track,
such their containment of forward thrust
I marvel that glass, and frame, don't crack.

Terrains

The names of the great logging barons still reverberate
the length and breadth of the States they made their own
in the institutions called after them, the lettering chiselled

on their ostentatious tombs. The jobs they provided
boosted the economy of the region: vast sawmills,
loaded barges heading downriver, a new dispensation.

The flip side: most were in it for what they could get:
nor philanthropists but cigar-smoking double-dealers
and land-grabbers, their pleasure lay in stripping it bare.

Then their pile made, departure; their legacy a structure
bereft of a core, perpetuating their names a deceit,
there having more often than not been no endowment.

As for what's left…remnants of pine forest, scant
cover for man or beast where formerly convoys
of wagons required lanterns in the middle of the day.

When extracting riches from a territory
every bit as open to pilfering and plunder –
the desirous expanses of the heart's terrain –

let poet and lover, eager to enjoy and employ
others' affections in conjunction with his own,
bear in mind what must be bequeathed in return.

Down the Years

High-stepping it through her College days,
former belle of the ball, habituee of soirées,
she later withdrew to a life of rural ease.

Little gleaned, other than emigration
and marriage (her first, his second)
to a wealthy breeder whose fortunes declined.

Inklings of tensions, 'all down the drain';
but nothing to home in on – hence our assumption:
a life of dawn gallops, verandahs, pink gin...

Till a boy with her colouring and pert nose-tip,
backpacking his way round Europe,
appeared out of the blue on our doorstep.

His teddy-bear mascot and blond muscularity
signalling an ambiguous sexuality,
over dinner he regaled us compulsively:

the first wife had shot herself; early on
his father thrown from a horse, damaging the brain;
bankcruptcy, loss of the land. To fend off violence,

they had to conceal the old man's firing-pins.
Finally committal; only for him to bend
the bars of his bed-rail with his bare hands.

Her love down the years, beyond
devotion to duty, beggaring description;
in return, no glimmer of recognition.

At whatever cost he is still the man she married:
a sacrifice the inverse of that endured
by Polyxena – head bowed to the blade, and doe-eyed.

(Polyxena, daughter of Priam and Hecuba, was sacrificed on the tomb
of Achilles to ensure the Greeks fair winds for their homeward voyages
after the fall of Troy.)

La Traviata

Violetta gives her final cry of joy,
then collapses. As the curtain falls
I picture two friends in their eighties,
she at home in the throes of illness;
he in hospital, hoping he will return.
Bravos over, a row of schoolchildren
show incomprehension: 'What was it
she had?' 'Cholera was common then.'
How convey the mores of the age,
the Baron duelling with Alfredo,
the demi-monde of the courtesan?
Time enough for pain and separation
to come their way. I sense a guilt
and trepidation at being spared so far
what our friends have undergone. How
differently art and life portray severance.
Tomorrow night, Violetta will die again.

Young Huntsman with Falcon
by the Maître du Jugement de Pâris de Bargello

Poised rather than posed, the central figure
glows amidst boscage. An outstretched wrist
eased of tension through the falcon's release,

one hand could be holding an invisible wand.
His frilled tunic seems not simply weightless
but so translucent it might be lit from within.

A foppish dog in mid-prance creates a sense
of a tranced forest: tempting to picture, beyond
the golden frame, the unhooded hawk transfixed.

As for the work which gives the artist his name,
if lost or destroyed, and the harmony and grace
of its goddess of love reduced to ghostliness,

why not in your ardour counter their absence
by superimposing the features of your beloved,
the warmth of her smile, modest tilt of her head:

though further reminders of impermanence,
each is rendered more precious and intense
through our acceptance of its transience.

Ways of Seeing
(for Rosslyn and Iain MacPhail)

I

Eight massive pillars support the octagon
of Ely Cathedral with its soaring lantern –
two hundred tons of lead, glass and timber
which seem to hang in space, light pouring
to the nave below; the life-sized carving
of Christ in Majesty drawing us upwards
toward Him, while our feet stay solidly
on the earth. On the floor of the choir,
a brass commemorates George Basevi,
architect of the Fitzwilliam Museum
who in 1845, surveying the west tower,
inadvertently stepped back into thin air;
his descent, releasing his soul instantly,
instigating a precipitate state of grace.

II

After the glory of King's, the grandeur of Trinity
I have a soft spot for the red brick of Robinson
which unlike these owed nothing to princes
but was the gift of a self-made millionaire
who, starting in his father's bicycle business,
was too reserved to attend the opening.
The lucent greens and blues of a Piper window
emblazon the east wall of its simple chapel –
but with the sun's effulgence so screened
that I whisper to the friend showing us round,
'What a pity, not to be able to share
from here the glory of the stained glass.'
Her reply both revelatory and salutary:
'Yes you can – if you are on your knees.'

In the Basilica

Despite swarms of Japanese
tourists, and solitary
devotees, the vast nave
preserves points of stillness

as where two nuns in grey and white,
one shy-looking, the other
angular and austere,
fragilely face the light

from the east window. A squat
man in a lumber-jacket
takes their photo: click,
then hands the camera back.

At this point
we take in the stain
of a strawberry-mark
stretching from chin to cheek.

I look quickly away
for fear of catching his eye,
but he is oblivious of me;
in his expression fleetingly

an intensity I've rarely seen,
part imploring, part trepidation
as though in this holy setting
he awaits a miracle happening,

a lifetime's imperfection
restored to freshened skin.
Unhurried, the grey
and white figures slip away.

Ministrations

The ghosts who haunt us
are not those who belong
to our superstitious past

or to childhood fancy,
gliding unconcernedly
through solid walls, clanking

chains in dank corridors
or descending stairways,
their heads in their arms.

Equally white-vestured
they are the apparitions
who will rise ahead of us

bearing pills and bedpans,
holding our hands
in unfamiliar rooms;

in gauze masks attending
during the operation,
helping to alleviate pain;

then when the day comes
drawing the sheet finally
over our flaccid faces.

Upon which it is we
who will dissolve, not they.
Best believe in them.

The Holy City

The concentrated aerial bombing of Clydebank on the nights of 13th and 14th March 1941 left only seven out of 12,000 houses undamaged. The glow from the flames could reportedly be seen from as far away as Aberdeen; and the tragedy and heroism resulting from the raids have passed into the collective memory. This poem was commissioned by the Clydebank Blitz Memorial Committee.

It stood, a skeletal sculpture on its hill
slope, a ridge of crumbling catacombs,
or as though a citadel fired in a great kiln
had been smashed at random; the flat
roofs that led to its name, the sunlight
on their rainy surface evoking Jerusalem,
reduced to a crude, charred honeycomb.

That name harder earned, through
the loss of those unhoused there;
distinctions of religion and politics
forgotten; grief and bereavement
shared with all of Clydebank, these
shattered tenements, debris-strewn
streets and terraces a communal shrine.

This adding dimension to the term
"Clydebuilt", conjuring up not the great
ships launched from here and circling
the globe, but the durability of ordinary
folk, stunned and taking to the hills, yet
stubborn in the face of whatever fate
might bring, any thought of overthrow.

Little notion then of the destruction
that would bring the War to an end;
the unveiling of a roll of honour
to civilians killed by enemy action.
The future unforeseen: Germany again
an industrial force; spacemen landing
on what had been a "bomber's moon".

At home, regeneration despite decline;
the yards closed, the Singer factory gone.
A new skyline – though still the presence
of ghost children, memories to preserve
for generations to come; and however
arduous the life ahead, sustaining
their resolve, that spirit of endurance.

Girl in a Picture (1927)
(for Cleodie Mackinnon)

She dominates your stair-well, brightly lit
and so fresh, she might have been painted
yesterday. No more than ten or eleven
she sits hunched, in a mauve skirt

and white espadrilles, her hair a tousle
of brown, girlish legs bare. The longer
we look, the more obdurate she appears;
in the alert features a farouche frown

as she refuses to meet the eye. Has she
the makings of a feminist rebel? To what
would she be driven, in later years?
We learn that having married young,

her officer husband was posted abroad
at the outbreak of War. Her parents
refusing to take their child, all three
embarked on a troop-ship for the Indies.

An hour out of Liverpool the captain radio'd
that they were being shadowed by enemy
submarines. Then all went dead. Nothing
heard of the vessel or its passengers again.

Kosovo

Milena

She lies at the edge of the pines,
black hair drifting over her face,
a silver earring sparkling;
alongside, her mother and two brothers,
one's arm bent over his forehead
as if still cowering from the bombs.

Among the rubble, in a childlike hand,
poems to a boyfriend: *Your Milena*
still loves you. If only you knew
how much I suffer. I feel my wounds so
I don't know if I can still kiss you.
In capitals in English, again: *I LOVE YOU.*

These lines and what they proclaim
all that remain as her body is loaded
on a dumper-truck and taken away.

The Hunt by Night

Figures run headlong through the forest
till all are brought down. At dawn
a great exhalation shrouds the marshes,
the meadows nearby. The beasts of the field
long since gone, the fowls of the air taken flight.

Ogre

We see on the screen daily
his puffy cheeks and white hair,
a man who has a price on his head.

To think he rises each morning,
does his ablutions like any other,
and passes out to the mundane air.

Disconcerting to have no sign: a malign
bubbling under the skin, or an insect
crossing the eyeball of the living man.

Hope

Think: in the depth of the forest
a source of light – only to discover
a tiny songbird, its plumage on fire.

The well

Arc-lights blazing they detect rotting
shapes, the stench unbearable: no
grapnel could pull them out without
fear of dismemberment.
                              Suggested:
Rope a gypsy, drop him down...

The inheritors

One dig unearths rows of corpses,
all male, heads aligned to the north;

Another, on the far side of the knoll,
centuries-old skeletons without skulls.

An eye for an eye, a tooth for a tooth.

'What can I do for Kosovo...?'

'I cannot offer hope, far less bring
loved ones back from the dead: so what
do I do?' Then it came to her: 'I can sing.'

A fund-raising concert ended
with a radiant rendering of some
of Bach's most sublime cantatas.

Envoi

A new millennium:
lavish parties, rapturous
tolling of bells.

Here, the dominant
sound still the thud
of the gravedigger's spade.

The Emigrants

On the long voyage south, families, herded intact,
were clenched knots of trepidation and sickness
buoyed only by belief that their journey, to almost
the limits of the globe, had to be finite, their new
world desperately one of possibility and hope.
On arrival the women and children kept aboard
while barracks built. Subsequent dispersal, further
settlements founded, hard work the key, a tenacity
to survive. In one community, such religious fervour
that when a respected divine died, the menfolk
fought for the right to carry his coffin, and no one
considered worthy to succeed him, his pulpit
remained empty for years. Hand in hand with which
all were determined to preserve another element
of their past, drifting into memory and dream.
This through folktales heard at a mother's knee,
songs passed down – helping those who had been
young children on arrival to retain early memories
of the big house with its iron gates and driveway,
coach-horses under chestnut trees; and indoors,
dimly peopled recollections of heavy curtains
and candelabras, in winter, icy kitchen quarters
lit by roaring fires. Their imaginings inducing
in succeeding generations a mistaken assumption
or illusion of ownership, expulsion to an unknown
country to start again; a spurious romanticism.
Imagine the shock, when a curious cousin's probing
into his distant ancestry revealed no such family tree,
but that they had been servants, not masters, all along.
This leading to ludicrous splits. Some in irritation,
even at such a remove, at what they'd no wish to hear,
resented being treated as victims of self-deception,
whereas imposture had not been the motive at all.
Others unsurprisedly accepted the discovery
that they were from a lower rung on the ladder
than they'd assumed or laid claim to. The enlightened
had the wit to see it for what it was, that to have risen
as they had was an accomplishment all the greater.

Meanwhile the stories and songs fervently passed down
stood them in good stead: a legacy in its way richer
and more durable than specious social position:
especially when, shifting fashion putting a fresh take
on oral history, they became the centrepiece of a book
attributing superior pedigree to those of peasant stock.

Distances

Planning an itinerary in the States, the table littered
with travel brochures, and puzzling where to stay
in Washington DC, we hear that kind friends – one,
his sight going – have made a booking in our name.
Only on touching down do we find we are immured
in a motel across the Arlington Bridge, trucks
rumbling on the freeway; the Smithsonian
a dingy cab run and subway ride away.

Each night I pace the drab confines of the room
or turn uneasily, the air-conditioning clanking,
thinking of bustling cafés and cherries in flower...
those stately thoroughfares. Much later, our
friends visiting, I ask churlishly why though
they knew we'd be sightseeing they'd chosen
that Day's Inn: turns out they'd thoughtfully
sought somewhere at not more than $100 a night.

That evening, seemingly apropos of nothing,
he tells how his father left when he was fourteen
and (his glass tinkling) that back then an ice-box
would've been a luxury. His mother bought him a blazer
in school colours, not realising they were worn only
by sportsmen, the showy badge sewn on: the worst
humiliation the day the football coach, offering him
a lift, found he wasn't a member of the team.

'That blazer lasted years, until frayed enough to be
thrown out.' He peers at a Book Festival brochure,
whose small print he can scarcely see. 'Did you tell
your mother?' Pale blue eyes unfaltering. 'Don't know
that I ever did.' Like a moment in a play, when the lights
dim or a gauze falls, hinting at some guilty intimacy,
lingering long after they've flown home to where they
can work out distances thriftily, for when his sight is gone.

Sightings

Leaving my varilux glasses on the plane
and hearing they have not been handed in
I wonder who else shares my vision,
the same precise distance from nose to ear.
I am also concerned at the expense. But more
positively, trust my carelessness may induce
some Tiresian insight, by way of recompense.

*

Just off the Ramblas, where we've been
repeatedly warned to beware of Moroccan
pickpockets, I give a squatting beggar
with a white stick and a tin mug between
his knees a wide berth. As I move on
my lasting impression is of dark glasses
and behind them, far from sightless eyes.

*

The Library through the wall from where
I am staying was once a medieval Hospital.
As I shower on my first night I hear
a juddering far below - a blind man
trying to make a getaway? At dawn
I peer out: the creaking shutters opposite
inch slowly up, like armadillos...

*

Topping the ceramic façade of Gaudí's
Casa Batlló, in the Passeig de Gràcia,
see zigzagging the spine of a dragon.
And as though clinging to a cliff-face,
balconies with railings of beaten steel
so curved the windows could be eyes
about to set out for a masked ball.

Postcards

Dropping them into a graffittied
postbox near the Palau de la Música
I realise all my cards have gone
without *Escòcia* on them: will they
reach Ayr, St Andrews, Orkney
under their own steam? Sent
likewise, carefully packaged,
would I make it I wonder
or at some dark border crossing
not know which way to turn?
Meanwhile those carefree
young couples oh so happily
cavort by the fountain – the logo
on their t-shirts: *'Go with the flow!'*

The Dragon's Cave
(for Anna Crowe and Miquel Desclot)

Setting out early from the Plaça
de Catalunya, our train journey
preceded the heady ascent
of La Mola. By musky evening
to have experienced not just
the fragrance of sage and pine,

the lattice-work of the valley,
Montserrat shawled in mist,
but through scaling the mountain
access to another culture. These
steps, expertly cut for pilgrims,
lead past a rocky outcrop

to the monastery at the summit –
its pantiled huddle, austerity
in stone. There we eat,
in an aroma of *fines herbes*;
a rarefaction for heart and mind,
a comradeship to treasure.

Since then our world, spinning
out of control, has seen
unleashed fiery beasts
more barbarous than that slain
over la Cova del Drac,
doing the innocents down.

Our thoughts as never before
turning to the safety of loved ones,
in calm recollection we cling
to such moments of exhilaration
as those shared, the day we were
privileged visitors, ascending in pure air.

II

Heirloom

Learning on moving house to Edinburgh
that my grandfather's licensed grocer's
had been in the High Street
made me feel less an interloper,
than one who has been long away.

Next door to the police station
he would leave out, on wintry nights,
a dram for the man on the beat.
And his special-constable's baton
bearing the city's coat of arms,

presented during World War One,
hung in our front porch for years
on its frayed leather strap, for decoration
but within easy reach in the event of intruders.
Only to end up lost, presumed stolen.

Growing Up

On Sundays I would take the boys to play
in Holyrood Park (we once had to knock
on the Palace door and ask for our ball back).
At that age the competitive spirit was high:

they'd fly into the tackle hell-for-leather
till I'd warn, 'Any more fouls of that kind,
we're off home', then have to stick to my guns
or lose face (*hoist* and *petard* come to mind).

Was this instilling a sense of fair play,
or simple abuse of power? I remember
the small group trudging back to the car,
the sullen silence throughout the journey.

Six-footers now, they're able to cope
with life's greater buffetings, take mature
decisions affecting themselves and others.
But I wonder, did their father ever grow up?

City Interlude

Rain stotts on the setts and bounces
from David Hume's bull-brows.
Outside the main entrance to St Giles

a young woman in a white dress
is lifted carefully from a wheelchair
and placed in the lap of a kilted piper

to have her photo taken. Their faces
seek the light. Then, the dress almost
transparent, she crooks an arm round

her male companion, who carries her
to a taxi that has been ticking over.
It drives off, raising a cloud of spray.

All this watched impassively by a pair
of wardens who now return to the fray.
The piper pumps his bag and starts to play.

Autumn Walk

Strolling through the Meadows
a few days after my birthday
I make the discovery
that advancing age has invested me
with a cloak of invisibility.
Close behind are two students. One,
her coat swinging open, displays
a bejewelled belly-button,
the other has hair like a pony's mane.
'I tell you, I waited and waited...
even turned over, lay on the bed
on my back. I can't make head
nor tail of him, after all the come-on.
How about you?' 'No problem,
the difficulty is stopping him
before I'm worn out. Have to find
you someone for the weekend.'
They head for the David Hume Tower,
their breath like plumes in the chill air.
I walk on, pondering growing old.
The leaves turn to russet and to gold.

Edinburgh Thaw

The snow sullied as quickly as it came,
already yesterday is like a frame

from a forgotten film. Closest to home
the flowering cherry in our garden,

no longer burdened by the weight
it bore, again flaunts its own white.

At street intersections, Christmassy figures
revert to being *Big Issue* sellers.

Uncannily, slush shifting on the bronze rider
in St Andrew Square makes him appear

to move – like Mozart's Commendatore;
while in the courtyard of the Assembly

Hall a pigeon, like a dove of peace, lands slyly
on Knox's upraised arm, and meets his eye.

Close Names

(for James Robertson)

Fishmarket Close and Fleshmarket Close,
preserved down the centuries, still
strike a chord; like Old Tolbooth Wynd
and the long gone Luckenbooth stalls,
their silver hearts intertwined; while
Hammerman's Entry summons
the bellows' roar, ring of iron on iron;
and Dunbar's Close, Cromwell's
Ironsides billeted after battle.

Sugarhouse Close and Bakehouse Close
boast their own past and function –
not quite Dippermouth and Porterhouse,
conjuring up images of New Orleans
cutting contests and tailgate trombones,
but suggestive of a distinctive music
resounding in the Royal Mile
throughout Scotland's history,
theirs a ground bass of a different kind;

now jaunty, the banners streaming,
now plucking the heartstrings
like the Blues, in the realisation
of things lost, the end of an auld sang.
As with the Blues too, a lingering
undertow of loss and deprivation:
the start of a new age – yet the city's
division into haves and have-nots
never more discordant than today.

Cappella Nova at Greyfriars' Kirk

Rare as whorls of gold-leaf floating in air
the cadences of Carver and the Inchcolm
Antiphoner are followed by the radiance
of a present-day elegy for Colum Cille –
he should have been Scotland's patron saint.

Emerging afterwards into a grainy twilight
(itself enough to make you catch your breath)
and walking past the domed tomb of bluidy
Mackenzie to where the Covenant was signed
it fully registers that the priestly composer

of another piece, all exultant counterpoint,
was Robert Johnston who fled to England,
charged with heresy, after the martyrdom
of Patrick Hamilton by Archbishop Beaton:
a torch which ignited the Reformation.

How swiftly beauty and horror intertwine,
the one so often a means of purging
the other; in this instance the singers
our intermediaries, the dark abyss bridged
by such poise...such perfect harmonies.

Coastlines

I rise early, letting you sleep on,
and go to see if the tall ships are in.
At Ocean Terminal masts appear
like arrows quivering in the haar.
Cramming the waterside at Leith
they make me catch my breath –
yet too shipshape and swabbed down
really to fire the imagination.
As I turn and push back through
the crowds, a pigtailed man in blue
jogs smiling by, pounding a drum
with his palms: dum-da-dum,
dum-dadum-dadum…hypnotically
that samba beat. Instantly
rummed bosuns dreaming of doubloons
run up the skull-and-crossbones
and head out to sea. A breeze fills
our vessel's full-rigged sails,
transporting us, young again,
to coastlines we have never seen.

Footage of RLS

Fade in. Opening credits over wreathings of haar;
then South Seas blue. Long shot of early removal
from Howard Place, though still within reach of the effluent
Water of Leith. Cut to the grandeur of Heriot Row.
Later in flashback, the fevers and forebodings
which presaged so much of his writing; that hacking
cough banishing him to the Land of Counterpane.
Subliminally in the background, Blind Pew tapping.

Aerial shot of the Pentlands. Dissolve to the Cévennes
where under starry skies he declares his desire
for the woman he would marry. Clips of their Silverado days,
his 'mountains of the moon', the icy cage of Davos.
Superimposed on cascading pieces of eight, a ghostly
hand writing to satisfy his daemons and foot the bills
for the hangers-on with their fancy tastes, that wastrel
Lloyd. Drifting in and out of shot, his 'dusky tiger-lily'.

Jekyll and Hyde are playing in an adjoining auditorium
(on split screen of course). Rushes of Weir of Hermiston
litter the cutting-room floor. The life he is enacting
smacks increasingly of a fiction. The publicity stills
no longer have him coughing up blood (bad for business)
but gazing enigmatically out of frame, except for one
where he soulfully eyes the lens. By the third reel
he seems to be yearning not for Belle (the B movie)

but for Allermuir and Caerketton, places he knew
he'd never see again, his Edinburgh long gone, so many
poems and stories written for the shadow of the child
he had been, part of a magic-lantern show; the dandy
and buccaneer in him exhausted. For the final scene
a double must have taken over: those grieving Samoans
hacking through jungle to lay him to rest on Mount Vaea.
The lights come up. He sits smiling at the back of the cinema.

Cornwall Landscape

The poet or painter steers his life to maim
Himself somehow for the job. His job is Love...
        W.S. GRAHAM

On his last appearance in Edinburgh
he started off by asking all those
who loved him to raise their hands;
an edgy Nessie whispering, 'For
goodness sake get on with it, Sydney.'

We sensed behind the plea a desperate
need for reassurance, for some sign
that his affection for his dear
(dead) loved ones was requited
in the land he'd left years before

and where the grouse calling go
back, go back can really mean it.
So he stood, rocking slightly
as if against a stiff sou'westerly
but somehow out of his element.

Now having holidayed not far
from his former cottage in Madron,
driven past Lanyon Quoit to Zennor
and stroked the mermaid on her stone,
we have seen above Botallack a buzzard

rising from a fence-post. And each
time emerging from those narrow
lanes banked with wildflowers, we
glimpse another Engine House jutting
from its rock-platform on the skyline:

Ding Dong or Levant, its new boiler
steaming, others restored as memorials
to disasters such as that at Wheal Dree
where '19 men and a lad' drowned
in the flooded tunnelling. The mineral

veins exposed by millions of years
of erosion, to induce such labour,
exact such a toll. Still common to all,
wherever we turn, the adjacent
brick-stacks, arms stiffly upraised

like an attempt at affirmation
in the face of time's attrition. And
even as we watch, in a thermal
high over the Duchy, a pair
of honey-buzzards soar and soar.

Think Tank
(for Gus Ferguson)

Though poetry readings can be hell
I pleasurably recall
your aplomb at Cape Town's
Two Oceans Aquarium – the audience
mesmerised as a gorging mass
of halibut, golden carp and sea-bass
passed behind you, left to right,
in sub-aqueous half-light.

We sat all ears but heads a-swivel,
as though in thrall
to a giant autocue: just think,
if someone could have miked the tank,
we might have learned what impression
its gawping denizens
had of ourselves, those curious creatures
on the other side of the glass...

Epitaph
(i.m. G.R.)

Having died on stage as Vladimir
in *Godot*, may his spirit appreciate
the twist of fate whereby the wait –
at least for him – is now over.

Writer's Block

Various ploys advocated to keep at bay
this beast they say can induce frenzy.
Some try 'hot writing' – like swimming
underwater…not coming up for air.

For stimulation one troubled troubadour
set his loved-one naked on a divan. Keats
put on his best shirt and shoes. Wordsworth
bemoaned its *long continued frost*. It made

Conrad want to howl and foam at the mouth.
Samuel Johnson didn't beat about the bush:
*A man may write at any time, if only he will
set himself doggedly to it.* Nearer our day

Gore Vidal takes the biscuit: *Something
I've never experienced. First coffee.
Then a bowel movement. Then
the muse joins me.* What more to say?

III

Ghosts at Cockcrow

Once, on this earth, once, on this familiar spot of ground, walked
other men and women, as actual as we are today, thinking their
own thoughts, swayed by their own passions, but now all gone,
one generation vanishing after another, gone as utterly as we
ourselves shall shortly be gone like ghosts at cockcrow.
>   G.M. TREVELYAN,
>   An Autobiography and Other Essays

Appearances

As the train draws out, the man seated
in front of us meticulously places
his jacket on the rack, opens his briefcase
and settles to a sheaf of papers, oblivious
of the mobile phone opposite, its owner
signing off loudly: '*bisous, mon cœur*'.

Designer glasses gleaming, body
language assured, he could be an *avocat*,
a partner in an art gallery, even a *député*
commuting from Paris to his constituency.
Though something trim and lithe belies
the customary trappings of the good life.

Then I notice he is poring over exam papers
on 'English comprehension', neat hieroglyphs
filling every available space in the margin
before he totes up the underlinings, gives
a mark, shuffles the pages and moves on.
He keeps at it, schoolmasterly, head down.

On our first morning in Dijon, the Hôtel Buffon
offers a pleasing precedent: how of the Comte –
in Drouais' portrait trig in embroidered waistcoat
and powdered wig, and looking for all the world
the *grand seigneur* – David Hume said 'he looks more
like a marshal of France than a man of letters'.

Notre-Dame, Dijon

The Cathedral's capitals look down
unperturbed, their carved features
interchangeable with today's
albeit more eroded, eyes less focused
than our own on the diurnal routine.
Outside, remnants of smashed stone
reiterate what these blind eyes
might have seen: not in this instance
destroyed like so many, during
the Revolution, but subject to a fate
as wanton as it was arbitrary:
a gargoyle, falling from high
on the main tower, flattening
a passing money-lender. This,
in a city like most others teeming
with usurers, a bad move. With little
love for the Christian society by whom
they felt excluded, the remainder
got together and using their hated
powers, had the rest hacked down.

*

In the wake of visiting cathedral after cathedral,
absorbing the glory of tympanum upon tympanum,
the depthless blues and rich reds of rose-windows,
two images cling from the *église* Notre-Dame: one,
of the wooden Virgin (claimed the oldest in France)
so badly damaged at the time of the Revolution –
arms and legs hacked off, the Christ child gone –
she is draped in a white sheet (and wearing a crown
of glistening gold); and as we leave by the great
west front, of a drenched mendicant in green
who, sensing our approach, lifts the heavy latch
and holds open the oak door for us to exit –
then with a twirling half-bow, accepts the small
change he is given, with a smile not quite right.

Musée des Beaux Arts

A row of terracotta figures
on fluted pedestals convey
an astonishing immediacy
of head-tilt and expression,
their setting and wig-styles
the only visual giveaway
that they are not of today.
That...and arguably
a dominance of eyeline,
an aura of hauteur, over
the assembled hoi-polloi.

*

Above the tombs of the Dukes of Burgundy
in the *Salle des Gardes* hangs a tapestry
depicting the raising of a siege by the Swiss,
the square tower at its centre visible today
from the windows of an adjoining room.

But what catches the eye is the vast effigy
of Philippe the Bold and his consort, supported
on all sides by a stooped procession of mourners,
cowled heads drooping over marble lineaments,
mortality rendered in all its implacability.

For such a memorial to be ready on time,
its decorative carving necessarily begun
many years before the Duke was finally taken.
A double burden: theirs an unknown deadline;
for him, a race it would be no joy to win.

Entracte

Biting into my roast rabbit
(*spécialité régionale*) I feel
a gold onlay loosen. That night
a cusp breaks off an upper molar.

Visiting my dentist whenever
I get home, will I discover
a cracked column and capital,
or crumbling nave and choir?

Hôtel-Dieu, Beaune

As not uncommon when a Treaty is signed, the end
of the Hundred Years War brought squalor and famine,
brigands and wolf-packs savaging those too weak to resist,
the onslaught of plague compounding the devastation.
Hence the founding of this spacious palace for the poor
(a monument too, to the donor's spiritual pride…?);
under barrel-vaulting, parallel rows of four-posters,
cross-beams jutting from the jaws of painted monsters.

Sacred artworks abound; and in a dim-lit chamber
a massive altarpiece depicts Christ the Conqueror
and the Weighing of Souls, St Michael's scales
consigning blessèd and damned to Heaven and Hell.
Certain instruments in the pharmacy amuse tourists
who in dumbshow enact their enema-function.
More fondly elsewhere, red bed-hangings bear
among turtle-doves the initials of the two patrons.

The *hospice* roof, its tile-patterns interlaced,
supports weather-vanes like pennants which stir
in the ghost of a breeze. And this the heart
of Burgundy, traditionally on the third Sunday
of November, the wine-harvest still auctioned
to sustain the "*pôvre*". Emblem of temporality,
a candle lit to start the bidding; when it gutters,
the proceedings are over for another year.

Vézelay

Our taxi-driver forgetting to come and collect us
for the ten-kilometre return journey to the nearest
station, our dismay at the thought of having to apply
luggage-less to some *chambre d'hôte* was wholly

at odds with the earlier discovery
that in the days when this had been a stopover
for penitents and pilgrims on the road to Compostela
hundreds slept rough, each yard of the street for hire.

Hotels

In each one, we are no more tangible
to the other residents than they to us:
muffled closing of doors, disjointed chatter,
hasty release of water in the small hours;
at dawn a clatter of keys, crunch on gravel.

*

At 2 a.m. I look out. The window directly
across the courtyard is unlit. Then
by an invisible hand, in the half-dark,
its net curtain is drawn slowly back.

*

Here each room has, instead of a number,
the name of one of Napoleon's Maréchaux –
twenty-six in all, their grave features
reproduced on a set of key-medallions
and postcards purchasable from reception.

When asked if their military ghosts roam
the corridors, the *patronne*'s look hardens.
But early next morning, no window open,
our swagged curtains seem to billow in,
their tops resembling ruffs, the heads gone.

In Transit

Returning from Auxerre we meet
other expresses, every seat empty
or passing at such speed, their passengers
are rendered transparent: either way
ghost trains, crossing fertile Burgundy.

Ghosts

In Besançon's ramparted Citadel we are almost the sole
occupants of the Museum of the Resistance and Deportation;
the last rooms particularly harrowing, with their depiction

of cattle-trucks heading for the concentration camps;
last letters to loved ones, others offering to betray
members of the Maquis – over a hundred rounded up

and executed in these confines. Easy to believe
the spirits of the innocent are housed within these walls;
traitors and collaborators destined never to find rest.

*

Remote areas are possessed by the ghosts of those
who tilled the soil in an age more rural than ours;
who scraped a meagre living, then departed
for the city or endured the *démembrement* whereby
family plots of land underwent constant subdivision.

Earlier, romantic figures always just outwith personal
recollection but vouched for, lodged in folk memory;
a fantasy people who lived in harmony and piety,
a Golden Age when each landowner served the poor
out of the goodness of his heart, and his own coffers.

*

Change discernible, in the sounds of the countryside.
Village clocks strike the hour twice. The occasional
creak of a hand-cart. Shrill cries of children;
click-clack of *pétanque*, under the chestnut trees.

In the pastures, still the creamy Charollais.
But fewer horses' hooves. An absence of song-birds.
And strikingly, none of those farmyard fanfares
which heralded daybreak, then punctuated all hours –

not just part of the rural fabric, but symbolic of France
since before the Revolution. Strange were these
to become a thing of the past, their raucous *cocoricos*
remote and irretrievable as our fugitive desires...

IV

ROULL OF CORSTORPHIN

He has taen Roull of Aberdene,
And gentill Roull of Corstorphin,
Two better fallowis did no man see
Timor mortis conturbat me.

WILLIAM DUNBAR,
'Lament for the Makars'

There is a poem in the Bannatyne Ms called Rowll's cursing…
Lindesay also mentions ROWLL; but there is no distinguishing
between the two poets of that name.

Sibbald's Chronicle of Scottish Poetry, Edinburgh 1802

Brissit* brawnis and broken banis,	*burst*
Strife, discord and waistit wanis,*	*homes*
Crookit in eild,* syne halt withal –	*age*
These are the bewteis of the fute-ball.	

ANON,
'The Bewteis of the Fute Ball'

58

1 Roull Posited

Whilst out hunting King David, separated
from his attendants, was heavily thrown
and about to be gored by a hart *with auful
and braid tyndis* – whereupon, a cross
placed miraculously in his hands, the beast
fled. He endowed an Abbey on the spot
with the *holy rood*; later, on a narrow
isthmus, founded the chapel of CORSTORPHIN.

A *sair sanct for the crown* maybe, and more
Norman than Scot, but for all that 'father
of the fatherless...best of all his kind'.
From then on the monks fed the poor;
where three centuries later Adam Forrester,
twice provost of EDINBURGH, would lie
in effigy, arms crossed, his armorial
bearings three buffaloes' horns stringed.

Could Roull have taken holy orders here,
catching carp or brewing ale for the brothers;
penning verse from matins to compline,
at the last, to drown in the brimming lea?
Or did *'gentill'* denote a patient dominie
instilling through Wyntoun's *Chronicles*
pride of nationhood, a concept of chivalry
in many later to be slain in battle?

No way of telling if he was a plague victim
or survived to old age; extolled his
mistress in royal-rhyme stanzas or caught
nature in cantering couplets. Yet that one
naming by Dunbar enough to make him –
allowing for the trudge from the Castle,
the cleansing Water of Leith between –
the capital's earliest recorded poet.

2 At Court

What a flyting in the Great Hall: Dunbar
kicked off, then Kennedy took the bait.
First one declaimed, the bit between his teeth,
then the other, even gustier than before,
each raucously varying his angle of attack:
it was as if the ground under our feet shook.

In masterly metre, Dunbar dazzlingly derided
Kennedy's cack-handedness, in surely one
of the most sustained swathes of mockery
and contumely ever, so cutting you'd expect
his victim to run off whimpering, tail between
his legs. Not a bit of it: back comes Kennedy,

switching tack, comparing his fine lineage
to his antagonist's (not without blemish),
and defending his renegade *Heiland tongue*
against Inglis. In retaliation, a fireworks
display so coruscating as to seem diabolic,
setting off a cacophony of shrieks and guffaws.

Just as they seem about to come to blows
(mere fisticuffs, after this, an anticlimax)
his Majesty steps forward, declares honours
even. Perspiring, Dunbar grins. Kennedy
lifts a leg and unleashes a prolonged fart
which is instantly declared *hors concours.*

Meanwhile Roull, of a gentler school
and ill at ease with such crudities,
side-stepping the toadying courtiers
slips out and heads back to Corstorphin,
where in the shade of a seeding sycamore
he will sit penning his tender love poetry.

3 To His Cousin in Aberdene

I retain mellow memories of your visit
and of learning much from you, anent
metre and rhyme. And seeing as I do
poetry's prime purpose as the interplay
of nature and the affections, trust in return
you will elevate your subject-matter:
I'd hate future exchanges between us
to degenerate into flytings, even in fun.

As to health, I hope neither of us will require
the visitor whose repertoire takes in the severing
of limbs and opening of the body's cavities:
diet of sweet herbs rather, to ease our ageing.
That is to say, despite rubbing shoulders
with Physics and Barber-Surgeons, I aim
not to let them practise on me – but quietly
to pursue my chronicling of the seasons.

And in an indeterminate age (heather-clumps lit
to keep my house decontaminate) give thanks
for a loving wife's contours, sons grown
to manhood; content here at Corstorphin. From
a nearby doocot, a constant whoo-whoo-ing.
As for immortality: the Makars' flowering
ensures our generation will never be forgotten,.
timor mortis non *conturbat me...*

4 His Cousin's Reply

Delighted to hear there is life
in the old dog yet, your wife
a sweet haven for your
desires. Have no fears
regarding my verse: the great
Dunbar I too prefer when aureate.
But high on my list, such scoundrels
as steal my capons and fat fowls:

Cursit and wareit be their werd*   *fate*
quhyll they be levand on this erd;
hunger, sturt,* and tribulation,   *strife*
and never to be without vexation...
povertie, pestilence or poplexy
I wish them, dum deif as edropsy,
the cruke,* the cramp, the colica,   *lameness*
the dry boak, &c. &c...

My stay vivid in the mind's eye,
several new poems at half-cock
describing the Castle on its Rock.
But I grew leery at the notion
of a royal tooth extraction.
Nor could I settle in Corstorphin:
after Aberdeen I need the sea –
its smash and sigh soothing to me.

But now I am home again
what hurts is the derision
of those who cry 'Butter fingers'
at my pig's bladder blunders.
How convey what hackers
they were who routed us?
But let them venture north,
by God we'll stuff them.

5 Roull on Musik Fyne

Nothing to the foul play of the choristers
at the Abbey of Scone. The worst,
sprightly loons who till we tackled them,
headed down each wing like a battalion
of demented gulls, cutting in on goal.
By the end, we were thrashed twelve-nil:
agile tenors in midfield, their last line
a bass-baritone built like a Scots pine.
All in all, despite our supporters' curses,
we had to admit they'd tanned our arses.

Later though, the radiance of their singing
in the Chapel Royal touched the heartstrings;
the Augustinian canon Carver, sturdy
enough to pass as *L'Homme Armé*
(and usurp the tune) transfiguring them
with his interweaving harmonies...
Lure them to Aberdeen, if they'll consent
to fight their way over the Cairn o' Mount
with its snow-swirls and snell nor-easters,
carrying their harps, lutes and tambours.

Is not our progress through life
a search for harmony, amidst darkness;
a blank parchment, awaiting the hand
to make of us an illuminated manuscript,
disponing both beauty and durability?
The King? He offers Carver commissions,
confident each motet will bring such balm
to his spirit as may help him forget
the burden of the iron chain he wears
as penance for his father's murder.

6 Insomnia

You say you can't sleep? By the doocot is the place:
under the eaves, the constant burbling of ring-doves;
and this the season for bees in the overhanging limes,
their lulling register between oboe and viola d'amore.

If that has no effect, try listing alphabetically
your favourite Saints: Adelaide and Aidan for starters.
The rocking of a moored boat soon induces slumber –
but not for sleep-walkers or the nightmare-prone.

With luck, a guttering candle will do the trick. Failing
which I wish you a clear conscience, the slumber
of the innocent. If that's too dull, the balmy haven
arrived at through impassioned hours of love-making.

7 Plaint

Under construction at Newhaven, to inspire terror
in any would-be invader, the *Great St Michael*
a triumph of the shipbuilder's art, two hundred
and forty feet long, bulwarks proof against shot –
and superintended by his Highness in person.

For this, every wood in Fife but Falkland
laid waste. And two hundred oak trees felled
for the hammer-beam ceiling in Stirling's
great hall. Lost for lifetimes to come. A marvel,
if one day we will have any forests at all.

8 Time of Plague

If I die first of us two, I'd rather
quietness than any ritual rend the air.

Nor any casting of ashes: on some high
hill we climbed, simply say goodbye.

And if beloved you be first taken
I'll do, however weakly, what I can

to treasure the living you. I'll try
in other words, to mourn with dignity.

But should either of these boys,
through mischance, predecease us

I'll hack out the God of Stone
and confront him with it – till one

of us lies broken, bone from bone.

9 To His Wife

The richest gift age can confer
is our growing old together,
not apart from one another.

But even more of a wonder:
loving you for what you are –
not just for what you were.

10 In Seiknes

If ever you do leave me, luve,
    'twill be a day o' dool.
The day that I leave thee, my luve,
    is the day I lie i' the mool.

For tho to leave this life we're laith
    I fear that day will daw
when in despite o' oor mortal aith
    the ghaistly cock sall craw...

11 Roull on Death

In the midst of *Life*, saith
the preacher, lurks *Death*:
yet still those who try
to bring it on more speedily.
Witness the Italian abbot
with whom James is presently
in thrall (among his promises,
to make gold from base metal)
who leapt from the wall
of Stirling Castle, only to fall
and smash his thigh-bone: his
excuse, that among the feathers
forming his wings were hen
quills which coveted the earth,
not the skies. All to counterfeit
King Bladud of old, who set
out decked similarly but took
a more grievous tumble, to
land on a temple of Apollo –
thereby breaking his neck.
No need to seek Death out:
the venerated Daubigny
on a visit to this country
sat at the King's right hand
at a tourney in his honour,
then collapsed in all his finery
while sampling our wine-cellars;
his blood, like best Burgundy,
a rampant tide. What a bustle
of ambassadors and courtiers.
His singular benefaction,
putting for a week Corstorphin
at the centre of the Universe.

12 Ghost of Roull

No poem of mine extant: would this were due simply
to time's vagaries, Gutenberg's revolutionary invention
supplanting the makar's flowery hand – if earlier,
I might have survived in manuscript form; later
through Chepman and Myller, preservation in print.

Even then such a debt to Bannatyne, not least
for Henryson's Fables – else unattributable,
those jewels in Scotland's crown; in their midst,
my cousin cursing whoever brak his yard and took
his hens: *blak be their hour, blak be their pairt.*

I still have his letters, stanza after stanza
on the reverse, blurred by candle-wax;
a fall putting paid to his seagoing and scavenging.
As for myself (ample scope to ponder since)
more likely lack of merit than Fate denied me

a drooling posterity, even as 'Anon'. At least
our presence in Dunbar's drum-roll of a Lament
(he outlived me little more than a year) confirms
our transient existence and that of our verse,
the whilk (for a spell at least) made readers rejoice.

Pursuing the *lilt of dule and wae*, hard how James,
having set himself up as a Renaissance
Prince, should have taken so many with him
at Flodden: one of Scotland's worst own-goals,
from a refusal to listen to the voice of reason.

Recorded that the Scots and English first tilted
at fute-ball at Bewcastle, Cumberland, in 1599:
one man disembowelled, but seemingly
sewn up again. Four years later, the Union
of the Crowns, a Golden Age bewilderingly

undone. Since then, rule by sword or pen;
pendulum swing of peace and war, amidst
the world's fears and turbulence. At home
the test, to this day, whether Scotland retains
the will to grasp the thistle, not the thistledown.

The Barber-Surgeons to King James IV

We the Barber-Surgeons of Edinburgh, gratified at the granting
of the Council's Seal of Cause, applaud your Majestie's probings
into the workings of the body, its ailments and cures. Neither
blood-letting, nor amputation and excision, lightly undertaken.
Yet the climate one of suspicion, witness Robert Henryson's
'*Sum Practysis of Medecyne*', scurrilously deriding *lechecraft*
and *feisik* alike – and by insinuation ourselves. Were we to wield
our instruments as he does his quill, the cleansing Water of Leith
would soon be the River Lethe. That said, as much quackery
in his calling as among our fellows: how many makars
worth their salt – most seeking truth through verse as likely
to find it up their erse. Mercifully not all tarred, with the one
brush…Were we the fraudulent cuckoo-spits he suggests,
we might belabour him with reciprocal curses. Suffice
to say his legal brethren in Dunfermline can keep him.
On another tack, Majestie, a modest plea. Pledged to honour
our calling in time of strife and plague, we are sore put upon
mending cracked skulls and broken shins from the fiery
pursuit of fute-ball. If not banned (or the worst hackers
booted out) could we humbly petition for a royal decree
preserving Holyrood Park for the more seemly sport of archery?

V

In the Museum of Scotland

I come across a white horse in a glass case,
decked with period artefacts each in its place:
saddle studs and plates, silvered harness junctions,
slivers of body-armour, and from muzzle to ear
ornate fragments of chamfron - not as a work of art
but displaying each item's ancient function.
Going to bed that night, I cannot but wonder
what of your "you-ness" might be deduced
from the strewn scarves, the array of bracelets
on the dressing-table, the jet and greenstone beads;
and what of custom and appearance, in those items
spilling from your wardrobe, could be implanted
in the mind of someone who did not know you.
My good fortune lies in having no need
of such accoutrements to conjure up
the warmth and gracefulness they enhance,
the living likeness of their milk-white steed.

The Tropical House

The Scotch pines seem close to slipping
their moorings - a home-grown variant
of van Gogh's crazed curlicues. Would-be

white-horses flecking the duck-pond, tiny
though it is, we scuttle for the sanctuary
of the tropical house. Instantly I break out

in a sweat, my specs steaming up so I can
scarcely see. But ideal for shelter: unlikely
even this gale will smash the glass dome in.

So we lean on the rail, study the water-
lilies in their pool, lotus and narcissus,
abundance of ease and innocence.

Till turning, we find we are hemmed in
by banks of serrated leaves, their spikes
tipped red as though daubed with blood.

Koi Carp...Kyoto

by Elizabeth Blackadder

Glazed but lit aslant, her Koi carp
enter our world from mysterious depths.
Left of centre the largest, blotched

orange and white, seems caught
in mid-plunge. Others flick their tails,
veer and pout, flaunt their colours,

gaudy geishas for whom existence
means eating, then being eaten.
Dusk falling, light-slivers quiver

on velvety fronds, ribbons
of jonquil thicken to gold,
cobalt to fathomless blue.

Part of me thinks back
to those days when the fear
was of falling into the latticed pond.

Another, conscious of fiercer currents
resists looking round, lest a dark shape
should come looming, jaws ready to snap.

Free Fall

At the time it was impossible to take in
the human dimension, until on the tv screen
the footage of those impelled by the inferno
into leaping to the sidewalk far below
showed one couple (work-mates or strangers,
we'll never know) share their last moments
swooping hand in hand towards infinity.

Mercifully we still have our loved ones.
But when in half sleep we instinctively
stretch out a hand to each other,
this so simple gesture of affection
is transformed: I shy from its reminder
of charmed lives; grief mingling with pity
for those who came hurtling through that funnel of fire.

Eclipse

The city spills light. But the moon,
in a clear sky, holds its own,
diaphanous and vulnerable,
a sliver of rime – till
full circle again,
the eclipse might never have been.
Tempting when all returns to normal
to forget what made us marvel,
or wonder if it really happened.
Back in bed, I slip a hand
gently across, touch your shoulder,
just to make sure you are still there.

Wayney and the Pink Tree
by Craigie Aitchison

Now ninety-three she remembers the street
since before we were born. Our flat
changed hands regularly; the earliest
occupant she can picture, a dusky woman
with a Ghanaian father, her eldest daughter
a silken blonde. Our front room boasted
a heavily draped four-poster, under layers
of dust: at the window, the dining-space.
But the sitting-room the *pièce-de-résistance*:
a tub with a tree in leaf – haven for damaged
birds, letting their broken wings mend
prior to release in the back garden;
tame ducks squittering on the floorboards
and for good measure a pair of red setters
to be fed and watered, given free rein.
Such odours and squalor mercifully long gone,
on the far wall we hang a silk-screen print
of three birds in flight and beside a tree
like candyfloss, a Bedlington terrier
transfigured by a wand of light. Whether
a Damascene conversion or symbol of canine
innocence, through these figures, so weightless
they seem to levitate, we consider the former
residents exorcised, their spirits free to soar.

My Lady

Increasingly I come to think of you not as my Madonna
of the Mountains, though that too in happy times, the air
crystal round you; nor my Lady of the Azaleas, Flora
of our city-centre sit-ootery though you undoubtedly are;

not primarily my Confidante of the Opera; nor despite
those heaped-up tomes, Queen of Quattrocento Art
and Sculpture. But at moments like this, my study right
over your kitchen, Diva of the Wonderful Smells. Saliva

glands drooling, I picture you amidst spice-canisters,
adding herbs to steaming casseroles, stirring in mystery
ingredients, reciting potions over bubbling tureens,
your cookbooks well-thumbed and worshipful as holy

writ. I imagine you moving so aromatically
from one cornucopia of culinary delights to another
that rather than concentrate as I ought on poetry
I end up pondering which wine is most likely

to enhance what we'll be eating, hoping you will permit
this indulgence, as a mode of saying *bon appétit*.
Afterwards my errant memory rightly earns the riposte:
'Why not add My Lady of the Binbag to the list?'

Change in the Weather

Listening on Radio Three to Dinu Lipatti
playing Mozart's Piano Concerto No. 21 in C
recorded over fifty years ago, shortly before
he died of Hodgkin's disease, I visualise
the view from your sickbed of snow patches

on Arthur's Seat. Beyond, sunlight glances
across the surface of the Firth. The matchless
serenity of the slow movement giving way
to those cadenzas which counter gravity,
I find myself willing your condition

to improve, if only by way of recompense
for what you have given others, down the years.
The music ends, the tumultuous applause fades.
The sun goes in, the coastline starts to recede.
And the crags reclaim their helmet of lead.

Coming of Age

In our day you got the key of the front door
at twenty-one, and everyone remained a virgin
until they'd left school. Try telling today's
teenagers that, they'll wonder what you're on.
But this was Kilmarnock in the 50s, long before
sex was invented (according to Philip Larkin).

Most of my friends' coming-of-age do's –
certainly the well-heeled ones – were out of town.
Before heading for the Plaza at Newton Mearns
we would visit Moss Bros, tussle with bow-ties;
while the girls came dolled up to the nines
in spangled ball-gowns, wearing heady perfumes.

More often than not the evening would be hell.
Heels hurting, I'd end up dancing with someone
no one else fancied, hope of romance fruitless;
the buffet a welcome respite, before eventually
the band would strike up 'Happy birthday
to you', and 'Never been twenty-one before...'

So to the last waltz, the dancers circling
and swaying under the spinning glitter-ball,
the fountains playing. A final mêlée,
then the bus journey across Fenwick Moor,
the couples at the back frantically petting,
others dreaming blearily of *'toujours l'amour'*.

Half a century later the survivors
prepare to pass on their inheritances
and amassed wisdom to their sons
and daughters; those early celebrations
occasionally surfacing, like flickering frames
from some old film, now almost forgotten.

State of Grace

(for Colin MacDonald)

Imagine, in my early Kilmarnock years
the Western Union Championship being won
at Kirkstyle, the last delivery of the last over
of the season hit for six by James Aitchison,
in those days, Scotland's opening batsman...

the ball caught by a boy on the long-on
boundary, then grabbed by someone
who ran off with it – to be found later
in a roll-top desk inherited by his son,
a dog-eared note confirming this as the one.

Counter-claimants: the youngster who swore
it was his grandfather who'd snatched it clean,
but saw it stolen; and a Riccarton policeman
who maintained the real one was handed in
shortly after, having lain hidden in a drain.

Not true. But suppose it had been. Given
the furore over the baseball that Bobby
Thomson hit into the stands for the home run
which won the pennant for the Giants in '51,
what would it signify? Surely not simply

that life in my home town, like any other,
was a microcosm of the world, but that even
in Killie small boys tried desperately to pin
down and hang on to the tremulous thrill
of those rare moments where the world stood still.

On the Slope

I cling to the railings as befits my station:
a senior person slipping slowly downhill.

The world no longer our oyster,
gone are the safaris of yesteryear,

the all-night parties, ice-skating
in the blurry light of dawn...

But perpetual youth? Think: the sense
of déjà vu, potions for complexion

and performance, the strain
of staying abreast of fashion.

Part consolation, the ungrudged ageing
of loved ones, neither left behind

but each meeting the other's eye,
enriched by what they've been through.

Whereas the mind roaming, and all
forgotten, pray for merciful oblivion.

The one sure adage: Bette Davis's
no-shit *'Growing old sure ain't for sissies!'*

The Hill Walkers

Accustomed to setting out under our own steam,
ham-strings tightening as the gradient steepens
(...Schiehallion, the Cobbler), then on the descent
our knees buckling, we have succumbed
to those telescopic trekking-poles all the rage,
to ease the weary slog of impending old age.

Today, not on the Ben but above Loch Lomond
we make light of snow flurries; on the way down
to encounter a thawing morass. The fun begins.
Our leader nose-dives first, his maestro's baton
describing a spectral arc. The second
flails fleetingly, a blind man in an abyss.

The sturdiest, poised like a skier at the gate,
instead of glissading down the piste
slithers out of control. Simultaneously
I do a back-flip, the quagmire under my feet
allowing just time – vain attempt at dignity –
for me to parry airily and cry *'Touché!'*

On the Summit

Having scaled Ben Vorlich and Stuc a' Chroin,
from above mist-level suddenly it was like seeing
Scotland unveiling: Ben More and Stob Binnein;

further west, the whaleback and scythe-like arête
of Ben Nevis. The joy of each summit,
its mastery a defiance of limits.

Not just Munro-baggers – many a Corbett
as tricky, no clear route marked out –
our unstated aim is to resist the onset

of age, or give that impression while
we can, aching limbs part and parcel
of a process testingly physical

at the time, then once home again,
triumphant in its reconstruction
after a hot bath, over a gin and lemon.

Best relive each moment for all it's worth,
before those photos of out of breath
gnomes in anoraks bring us back down to earth.

Piazza del Campidoglio

In the thirty years since I visited Rome solo
I'd looked forward to returning with you
and to your first glimpse of the Campidoglio,

by far the loveliest square I've ever seen.
For weeks prior to our going, I'd imagine
you climbing the steps then pausing to take in

Michelangelo's design, flanked by the Capitoline
Museums; smack in the centre the great bronze
of Marcus Aurelius on horseback, gazing down.

Only it turned out differently. Climbing
from the Forum meant our approaching
from the rear – somehow so disorienting,

such a marring of anticipated perfection,
as to be the shuddering of a fault-line. When
eventually I took your hand, something had gone

and I'd tarnished what I wished you
most to treasure, that first miraculous view
of a beauty which, momentarily, embraced you.

Once we were inside, mercifully
the wonder of the artworks on display
took hold – Cupid and Psyche's butterfly

kiss almost within reach of the Dying Gaul,
then the other rooms and corridors until
we were overcome by the glory of it all.

Can there be moments too precious to bear,
or an irrational undercurrent of fear
at having to preserve, for the remainder

of our days the convergence of a particular
time and place, like not spilling water
brimming in a vase, however

steep the path? Either way I love and admire
you, for your wonderment, all the more –
although I suppose there will linger

a disquietude that were we to arrive together
at heaven's portal (Elysium, if you prefer)
I'd most likely spoil that too, out of terror.

Witnesses

(for Lachlan MacColl)

Against a steady swell we cling to the lee
of an island, hoping to get our own back
on an intransigent loch that has so far yielded nothing.

Schoolmaster and jazzman, this your first trip
since leaving teaching. You trawl memories of those
to whom you gave so much over the years;

today both an ending and a beginning, a continuation
of their careers – and your own: who knows
what chords and improvisations to come?

The keel grates on gravel. Covering a rise you hook
a rainbow. Two red-breasted merganser tread water,
heads angled rakishly – then dive and disappear.

'Any joy?' 'A couple of two-pounders':
yours enough to win the prize, when we head in
to the boat-house to face the others' banter.

In bed that night I sense, heads erect, banded
white and chestnut, that pair of merganser;
the amazement, simply, of their being there.

Off the Water
(for Norman Kreitman)

After a blank day on Portmore as the guest of a poet
who was also a psychiatrist, muffing my final cast
I felt a stab as the barb bedded in my finger.

Through a ghostly luminosity we came off the water
and my host drove me to the Infirmary
where a trainee nurse snipped at the dressing

with tiny scissors, saying as I winced, 'My dad
used to push the hook through with pliers,
it happened all the time.' My manliness slipping,

my friend murmured 'I tried that, yes'. Finally
under local anaesthetic, the fly deftly removed.
I reached home determined to cast more carefully

in future – while blearily hoping the mishap
might give rise to a poem, though poems can be
slippery as a brownie or rainbow to land safely.

Now I'll send this to my angling companion
for his scrutiny: see him hold it to his eye,
analysing each line, testing its breaking-strain.

Prologue to *Hecuba*

(after Euripides)

Once was Troy: a walled city, naked
to the sea; its gateways guarded,
granaries heaped high. On its central
hill, a citadel of white stone:
the royal palace, where I was born.
For I am Polydorus, youngest son
of Queen Hecuba and King Priam.
In boyhood I competed with my brothers
and sisters. There was feasting
and dancing, laughter and song.
The compliance of Helen changed all that.
The Siege began. Too young to fight
I was sent secretly here to Thrace,
whose ruler had often been our guest.
With me for safe keeping, jewelled
coffers; a royal store of gold.
For ten years Troy was ringed by Greek
spears. So long as the city held out
I was treated as a son. Then the tide
turned. One by one my brothers
were slain. Hector, his ankles slit,
was slung from the chariot of the beast
Achilles and dragged in the dust
round Troy's walls. At last a huge horse
of mountain-pine bridled with gold,
a parting gift from the enemy,
was wheeled into the square – its belly
filled with armed men. That night
as the city slept, they crept out
and opened the gates. The Trojans
were slaughtered to a man; the women
tethered like cattle. My father,
clutching the altar-rail, was hacked down;
his palace ransacked. So Troy
fell. I became the last, of my line.
Maddened by gold-lust Polymestor my host
instantly had me slain, my body mutilated
and cast into the sea. The Greek fleet,

speeding for home with its slave cargo,
was hit by storm and put in here for shelter.
Now itching to be under way, they are impeded
by a flat calm. Past their beaked prows,
the hawsers littering the shore, I come –
the semblance of a man – to hover
over my mother Hecuba, Queen no longer
but taken into captivity; to forewarn her.
Looming over the headland, wearing
the armour in which he was buried,
there has appeared to the Greek force
the phantom of their hero Achilles
who fell in the last assault on Troy.
Not satisfied with a gold urn, the mound
raised to him, games held in his honour,
he demands my sister be sacrificed
on his tomb: then fair breezes will come.
Unable to straddle her, take her as booty,
he envisages this foul fusion of the blood.
Mother, do you think this is a dream?
That I am a voice inside your head?
I tell you, there has been such slaughter
our world is an abattoir, Troy a smoking ruin.
Children have been flung from its parapets.
Soldiers crawl over corpses, like blowflies
on meat. Now my sister is to be given up
to those cultured curs. Meanwhile, desperate
for burial, I loll in the shallows; my body
bloated, limbs half-severed, intestines
trailing like an afterbirth. Mother,
how can you sleep? Think what lies ahead.
You will have no rest until you, too, are dead.

The Actor's Farewell

It faded on the crowing of the cock.
Hamlet, I. i

Even in my heyday, I never played the Prince:
Horatio in rep, Laertes at school performances,
but never Hamlet in his black doublet and hose.
In contrast I remember the frisson of first striding
the battlements, in the glinting armour of the Ghost.

For a spell my speciality was not just doubling
but despite being stabbed behind the arras,
trebling as Polonius and First Gravedigger.
But that meant reappearing at the final curtain:
my preference, simply to vanish into darkness.

Even then I felt compelled to await heaven's
remonstrance; Hamlet mesmerised in his hall
of mirrors, driven to the rim of madness;
or from the safety of the wings, to watch Claudius
and his heartless queen get their comeuppance.

Whilst these and the others were drawn
from Holinshed or Thomas Kyd's tragedy,
the Ghost was purely Shakespeare's invention.
Each night I went on I sensed hovering round me
all those who had played the role previously.

Sometimes on tour things would go wrong:
once a rostrum not properly set, on my exit
I stepped into thin air; or some half-pissed idiot
missing his cue, a late *cock-a-doodle-doo* and thud
screwing up *'the morn in russet mantle clad'*.

But the great fear (ask any actor), my memory
going. Till a bright SM recorded my speeches
for me to mime to. Then one matinee the machine
went haywire; my jaws opening and closing
like a demented goldfish, to a frenzied whirring.

The derision of the gods, the last straw. That
and a director who reduced the Ghost's
presence to a trick of the light. Time to call it
a day. By then I was having second thoughts
anyway: didn't I trigger off the whole action...?

Mind you I learned not to overidentify
with my role (in my view Stanislavsky
could addle the brain); and despite
the skeptics, clung to the assurance
that Shakespeare himself believed in me.

The one lingering frustration
about which nothing could be done
was how in production after production,
despite resolution of the revenge theme,
Old Hamlet's soul remained unshriven.

As for the new minimalism, increasingly
I recall those gloriously costumed runs:
irrevocably gone, yet in spirit they remain.
The ultimate cockcrow? I'll be ready when
the time comes: '*Adieu, adieu! remember me.*'

Angel with Lute

High on the vaulting as though levitating,
for five centuries I have gazed down
at a blur of straining adam's apples,
gaping nostrils and goggle-eyes focusing
on the frescoes for long enough to take in
my soft colour tones, my wings' pale
transparency, my fingers on the strings.

Against the hair-line cracks in the sky,
faded through the ages, only traces remain
of my halo's gilding. But no disruption
of my features, thanks to my master
having properly prepared his pigments
before drawing my curls and straight nose-line,
the powdery red and green of my costume.

Not just the fee (though that filled his belly),
or religious conviction. I'll tell you a secret.
Invisible from ground level is a small smudge
on my cheek. His last brush-stroke complete
and before they dismantled the scaffolding
my master leaned up and kissed me gently.
After all those years, that still sustains me.